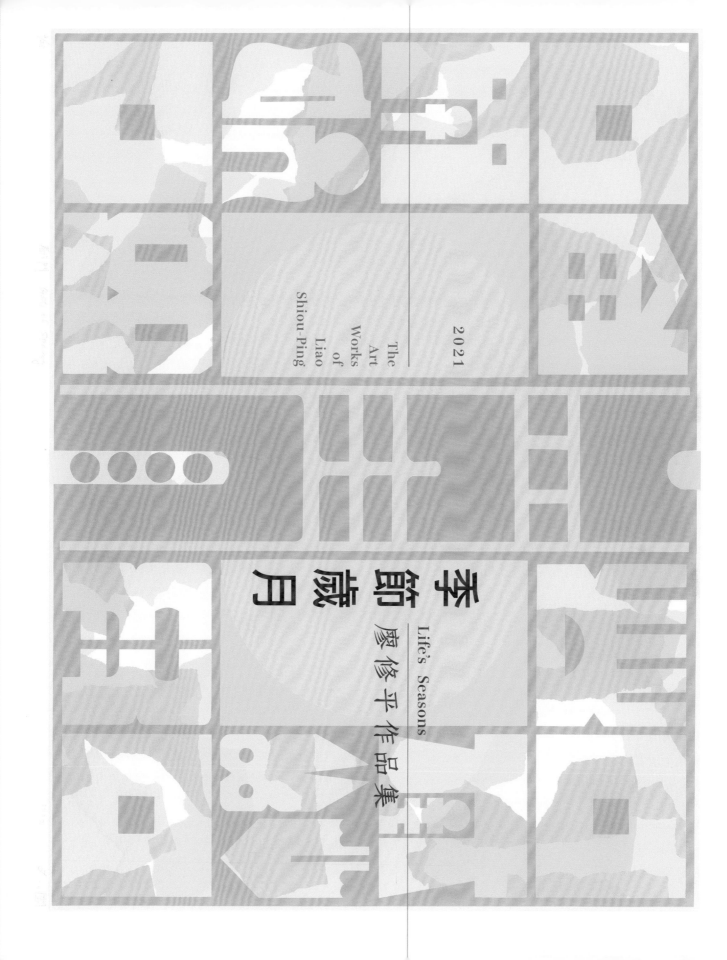

季節歲月

節

歲

月

廖修平作品集

Life's Seasons

The Art Works of Liao Shiou-Ping

2021

局長序

「版墨交融」－廖修平、黃淑卿雙個展

桃園這片土地孕育了無數富有創造力的藝術家。近年，更吸引許多桃園以外的創作者，以藝會友，相互觀摩，提昇人文素養，也為桃園傳承扎根藝文能量。「版墨交融」，即為臺北藝術家移轉藝文能量到桃園展支」以畫會友的代表之一，這是版畫創作者廖修平與水墨創作者黃淑卿在 2021 年的雙人個展，其中桃園景物亦以版畫與水墨兩種型態入畫，並呈現桃園之美。

廖修平以版畫創作榮復多項國際獎項，終生致力於版畫藝術推廣，享有臺灣現代版畫推動者的美譽。他以具東方美學韻味的創作，和台灣特色的符號系列，形成個人符碼，成功傳達台灣文化特色和獨特語彙。近 70 年的創作歷程，藝術家展現豐沛的創作能量，本次廖修平以「季節歲月」為展覽命名，展出以 80 年代到近期的「聯屏式」版畫創作，包含「季節」與「生活符號」兩個系列，再以桃園大溪老街、台北龍山寺等，創作出蝕刻版畫，十分具地方代表性的文化風情速寫。

黃淑卿，畢業於國立台灣師範大學美術系，為美術創作理論組（水墨畫）博士。喜歡畫、水墨創作、書法、藝術欣賞、生態賞及賞鳥等，畢生致力於藝術教育與生態藝術的耕耘。本次以「島嶼傳說」為展覽主題，以鳥類做為水墨創作的核心元素，結合台灣人文景觀、民俗文化及原住民傳統藝術的內涵，以多元視野的藝術觀點，創作媒材援引木印木版肌理為畫作形式與背架，來呈現當代水墨畫作中、自然生態、人文懷與多元文化共融的理想。

廖修平和黃淑卿兩位老師，活躍於臺灣藝壇，又旅行世界各地，長期推動臺灣版畫與水墨創作的國際見度，除了舉辦聯展和個展外，深耕藝術園地；本次展覽期待能與眾多桃園藝文團體搭建起藝術的橋梁，連結桃園在地萌芽的多元藝術文化能量，一起為桃園藝術文化的豐富而努力，特為文祝賀展出成功。

桃園市政府文化局長

Director's Foreword

"Fusion of the Printmaking and Ink Art"—
Dual Solo Exhibition by Liao Shiou-Ping and Huang Shu-Ching

The soil of Taoyuan has nurtured countless creative artists. In recent years, Taoyuan has also attracted many creative talents from beyond the city to interact and exchange with local art circles, further driving the cultural development and boosting Taoyuan's artistic energy. "Fusion of Ink Wash Painting and Printmaking" is one great example of Taipei artists' transferring of artistic energy to Taoyuan for "exchange with local art circles;" it is the 2021 dual solo exhibition by printmaker Liao Shiou-ping and ink wash painter Huang Shu-ching, as they also have created prints and ink wash paintings depicting the sceneries and local features of Taoyuan, presenting the beauty of the city.

Liao Shiou-ping's works of printmaking have won numerous international awards, and he has been regarded as the pioneer of modern printmaking in Taiwan for his lifelong dedication to the promotion of the art of printmaking. Liao's creative works depicting Oriental aesthetics and series of symbols representing Taiwan's unique features have formed his personal code, successfully conveying Taiwan's cultural features and unique vocabulary. Over his creative journey of nearly 70 years, the artist has displayed abundant creative energy. Mr. Liao has given this exhibition the name "Seasons and Time," which exhibits his works from the 1980s to the more recent "paneled" prints, including two series entitled "Seasons" and "Symbols of Life;" moreover, he has also created etchings of sceneries of Taoyuan's Daxi Old Street and Taipei's Lungshan Temple, presenting drawings of iconic local cultural sceneries.

Huang Shu-ching graduated from the Department of Fine Arts, National Taiwan Normal University, and has earned a PhD of Fine Arts Creation (Ink Paintings). She loves painting, ink painting education, calligraphy, art appreciation, ecological art and bird watching, and has dedicated her life to art education and ecological art. This solo exhibition is themed "Tales of the Island," where she uses birds as the core element of her ink wash paintings, combining Taiwan's cultural landscapes, folk culture, and traditional indigenous arts to form diverse artistic views for the realization of her dream of cultural fusion. Huang appropriates the texture of watermark woodcarving as the format and framework of her paintings, presenting topics of contemporary ink wash painting like natural ecology, humanitarian concerns and fusion of diverse cultures.

Both Liao Shiou-ping and Huang Shu-ching are active figures in Taiwan's art community, and have long travelled the world to promote Taiwan's printmaking and ink wash painting on the global stage. In addition to organizing group exhibitions and solo exhibitions, they have dedicated their lives to cultivate art in Taiwan. This exhibition looks forward to connect with the many local art and cultural groups in Taoyuan through art, linking the diverse emerging local artistic energies of Taoyuan to jointly strive for the richness of Taoyuan's art and culture, and I wish these two solo exhibitions great success.

Director, Department of Cultural Affairs, Taoyuan

Amy Chaang

自序

季節歲月

我，1936 生於台北。1959 台灣師範大學美術系畢業。1962 至 1968 留學日本國立東京教育大學及法國國立巴黎美術學院。1968 年底旅居紐約，2002 年返台定居。

在季節歲月流轉中，從進入師大美術就讀至今，近 70 年的創作時間，懷抱對藝術的熱情及理想，持續耕耘，嘗試不同的技法與接納來自世界各地的藝術觀念，對故鄉台灣的記憶情感，成為我創作的動力及靈感來源，這就像當我們走過無數變換不斷的四季人生，特別是在四季分明的歐美，當殘灰若冥的嚴冬一過，緊接著就是清新富朝氣的翠綠春意，滲著生趣益然的鮮黃；然後走過悶熱的炎炎夏天，就又到了光輝燦爛的深紅秋葉。這一葉可以知秋的季節，恰如人生邁上中年的黃金歲月。秋天，不正就是鉛華洗盡的年歲，也正是人生經歷萬千變化之後，逐漸豐熟的思想高峰。故這次以「季節歲月」為展覽命名，作品以 80 年代到近期的「聯屏式」版畫創作為主軸，版畫種類包括：紙凹版、絲網版與蝕刻金屬版。規畫展出三個子題：一、「季節」；二、「生活符號」；三、「捉影 Drawing」。

一．「季節」

走過無數四季變化，生命的時空，從台灣輾轉穿越巴黎、日本和美國，從六〇年代走到了二十一世紀，看盡季節的冷暖變化，也體驗人生四季的陰晴圓缺。常用「金、紅、黑、銀」來代表春、夏、秋、冬，述說人生的悲喜與離合。旅居他鄉，朋友相聚，無論是淺酌小聚或是觥籌交錯的暢飲，重要的是相聚的情誼，發展出以季節、景物、生活器物為題材的創作。將四季變化喻為人生過程，生命流轉、變化萬千，心境則隨緣，從和諧的境界中獲得體悟、昇華。如作品：1987〈山 湖 竹 I Ⅱ Ⅲ〉、1989〈窗（春）（夏）（秋）（冬）〉、1991〈敘園（二）〉、2021〈海岸（一）（二）（三）（四）〉等。

二．「生活符號」

將常民生活的物質文化轉譯成藝術符號，結合了現代繪畫的造型觀念和本土符號元素，創作具有東方精神和台灣民族特色的「符號系列」，作品中的符號，來自對美好人生的追求與祝福，形式根源於台灣民間祭祀用的金衣錢，日常生活中常用的剪刀、雨傘、梳子、謝籃等身邊親切的工具什物，配以居家的門、窗和男、女、衣、鞋等圖像，呈現豐衣足食而安詳的人間生活。

民間善用的吉祥紅色和豐足意味的金、銀箔，以簡潔的黑色、豐潤圓滿的線條、對稱方式的構圖，予人沉穩安定的感覺，意念上強調在繁複的現代生活中，隱藏著生生不息的自然秩序及充滿台灣節慶喜悅的趣味。如作品：2008〈雙福一二三〉、2012〈人生四季（一）（二）（三）（四）〉、2021〈季節（一）（二）（三）（四）〉等。

三．捉影 Drawing

人生歷程走過亞歐美，再回到故鄉台灣。創作從生活所感出發，融合當下生活旅行所在的人文在地風情，進行寫生紀錄，再以蝕刻版畫呈現桃園大溪〈老街〉、台灣〈龍山寺〉、巴黎〈聖母院〉等貼近生活情感的人文景致。

很榮幸於 2021 年 10 月於桃園文化局展覽廳展出，與熱愛藝文的朋友分享「人生四季・季節歲月」的真善美。

廖修平

Preface

Life's Seasons

I was born in Taipei in 1936. I graduated from the Department of Fine Arts, National Taiwan Normal University (NTNU), in 1959. From 1962 to 1968, I studied overseas in Japan and France at Tokyo University of Education and L'ecole des Beaux-Arts. I lived abroad in New York since the end of 1968, and returned to Taiwan in 2002.

As seasons and time go by, I have embarked on this creative journey for nearly 70 years since entering the Department of Fine Arts at NTNU; with great passion and aspiration for art, I continue to work hard, trying different techniques and embracing artistic concepts from all around the world. The memories of and emotions for my hometown Taiwan have become the source of my creative drive and inspiration. It is just like how we have gone through the constantly changing seasons in life, especially in Europe and North America where seasons are distinct—once the dark winter is over, what follow are the spring's refreshing and robust greeneries interwoven with the vibrantly fresh yellow; after the humid summer, we are greeted by the glorious and splendid red leaves of autumn, and this golden season is like the golden years in life during the middle age. Autumn, it is the time to shed vanity, as we have experienced the ups and downs in life and our minds have gradually matured and peaked. Thus, I have named this exhibition "Seasons and Time," which features mainly my works of printmaking from the 1980s to the more recent "paneled" prints, and types of prints include: paper intaglio, silkscreen, and metal etching. The exhibition showcases three subthemes: 1. Seasons; 2. Symbols of Life; 3. Drawing.

1. Seasons

Having gone through countless changing seasons and different times and places in life, I have travelled across Taiwan, Paris, Japan, and U.S., from the 1960s to the 21st century, and have seen the ups and downs through the seasons and experienced the wax and wane of life. I often use "gold, red, black, and silver" to represent spring, summer, autumn, and winter, telling the stories of gathering and parting in life. Living abroad, whenever friends gathered, regardless of over a drink or getting drunk, the most important thing was the bond that brought us together, which I have developed into creative works using seasons, sceneries, and daily objects as themes. I compare seasonal changes to the course of life; the journey of life is full of changes, and my mindset is to simply go with the flow, gaining realization and sublimation through harmony, just like my works Mountains, Lake, Bamboo I, II, III (1987), Window (Spring)(Summer)(Autumn) (Winder) (1989), Redenz Vous in a Garden (II) (1991), and Seacoast (I)(II)(III)(IV) (2021).

2. Symbols of Life

Translating the material culture of the lives of ordinary people into artistic symbols, I combine the graphic concepts of modern painting with the representative local elements of Taiwan to create the "Symbols" series that captures the

Oriental spirit and Taiwan's ethnical features. The symbols in the works are inspired by the pursuit and blessing of a beautiful life, and their format originates from the paper money and clothes used in folk rituals; common everyday objects such as scissors, umbrellas, brushes, and rattan baskets; the doors and windows of homes, as well as symbols of man, woman, clothing, and shoes, presenting an abundant, and peaceful life on earth.

Symmetric compositions are created using the auspicious red, as well as gold and silver foils representing abundance, often used by ordinary people, and smooth and round lines in clean and slick black, exuding a sense of calm and stability. The idea is to emphasize the hidden endless natural order and festive attraction of Taiwan within the complex life of modern society, such as: Double Wealth I, II, III (2008), Life's Seasons (I)(II)(III)(IV) (2012), and Seasons (I)(II)(III)(IV) (2021).

3. Drawing
My life journey has taken me to Asia, Europe, North America, and finally back home to Taiwan. Creative works are inspired by life, and I fuse and record the local cultures and customs of where I lived or travelled to at the time through drawings, and then present through etchings the cultural landscapes like Taoyuan's Daxi Old Street, Taiwan's Lungshan Temple, and Paris' Notre Dame, that reflect everyday sentiments.

It is a great honor to organize this exhibition at the Department of Cultural Affairs, Taoyuan, in October 2021, sharing with all the art loving friends the truth, goodness, and beauty of "Life's Seasons – Seasons and Time."

Liao Shiou-Ping

目錄
Contents

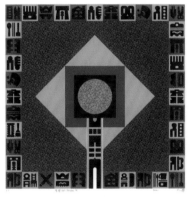

季節（一）（二）（三）（四）

Season Ⅰ Ⅱ Ⅲ Ⅳ

絲網版
Silkscreen
66×66cm ×4
2021

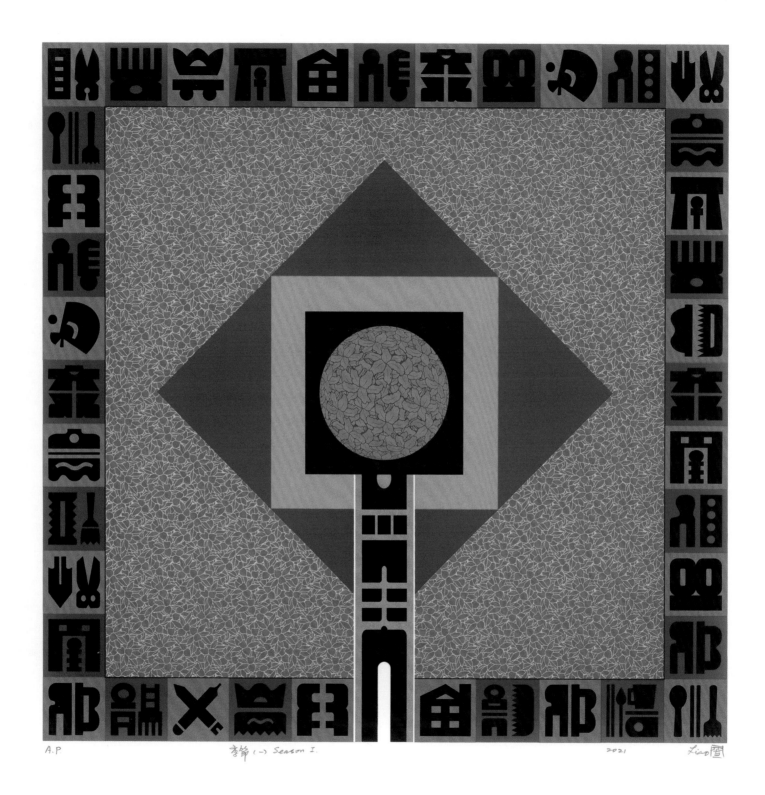

A.P   季節（一）Season I.   2021   Liao 廖

季節（一）
Season I | 絲網版 Silkscreen | 66×66cm | 2021

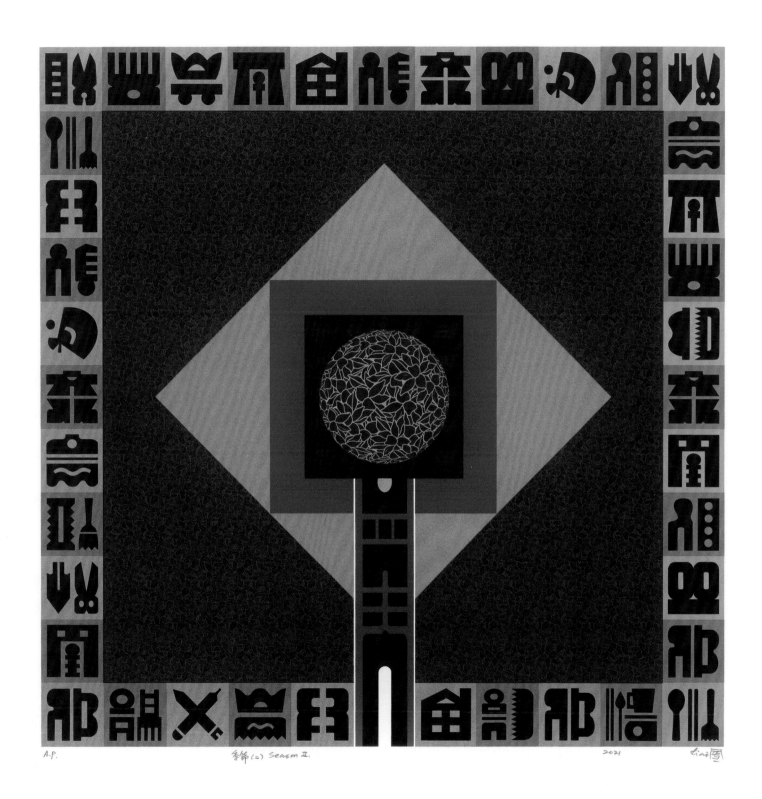

季節（二）
Season Ⅱ ｜ 絲網版 Silkscreen ｜ 66×66cm ｜ 2021

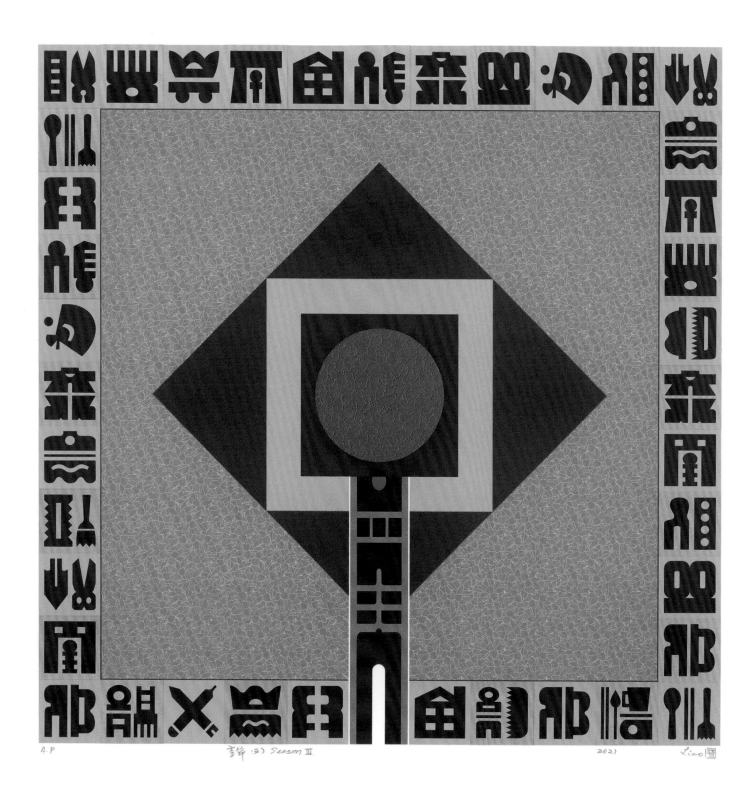

季節（三）
Season Ⅲ ｜ 絲網版 Silkscreen ｜ 66×66cm ｜ 2021

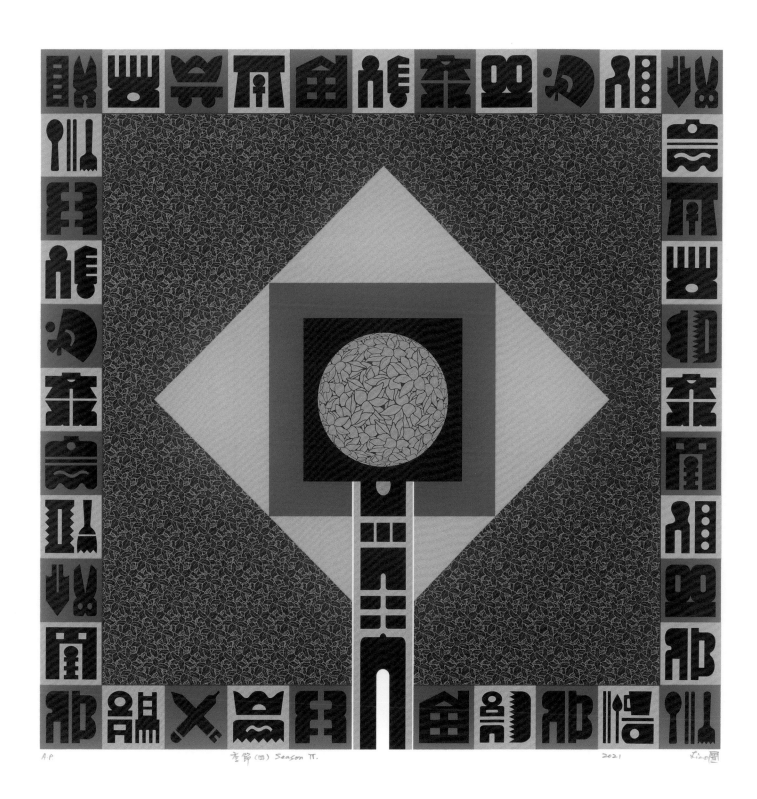

AP　　　　季節（四）Season IV.　　　　2021　　　　Lin 圖

季節（四）
Season IV │ 絲網版 Silkscreen │ 66×66cm │ 2021

海岸（一）（二）（三）（四）

Seacoast Ⅰ Ⅱ Ⅲ Ⅳ

絲網版
Silkscreen
66×46cm ×4
2020

A.P.　　　海岸 (三) Coast III.　　　2020　　　Liao 廖

A.P.　　　海岸 (四) Coast IV.　　　2020　　　Liao 廖

福祿壽之門

Gate of Fortune, Prosperity & Longevity

絲網版
Silkscreen
106×274.5cm
2016

proof   祿 prosperity   2015   Lim 圖   壽 longevity   2016   Lim 圖   林鴻春:林鴻春版畫藝術 prosperity & longevity 9786267020326 Lim 圖

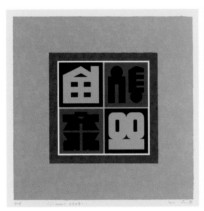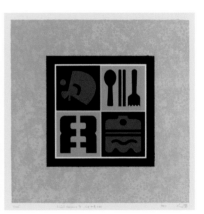

人生四季（一）（二）（三）（四）

Life's Seasons Ⅰ Ⅱ Ⅲ Ⅳ

絲網版
Silkscreen
58×58cm ×4
2012

人生四季（一）
Life's Seasons I ｜ 絲網版 Silkscreen ｜ 58×58cm ｜ 2012

人生四季（二）
Life's Seasons II │ 絲網版 Silkscreen │ 58×58cm │ 2012

人生四季（三）
Life's Seasons Ⅲ ｜ 絲網版 Silkscreen ｜ 58✕58cm ｜ 2012

人生四季（四）
Life's Seasons Ⅳ ｜ 絲網版 Silkscreen ｜ 58×58cm ｜ 2012

雙福一二三

Double Wealth I II III

絲網版
Silkscreen
87×150cm
2008

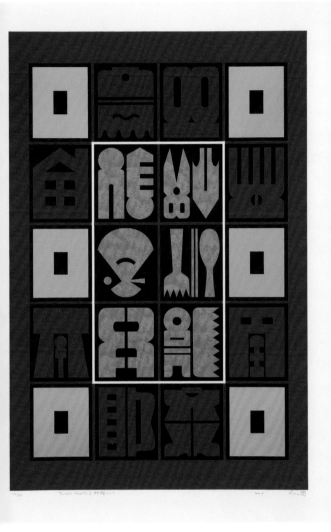

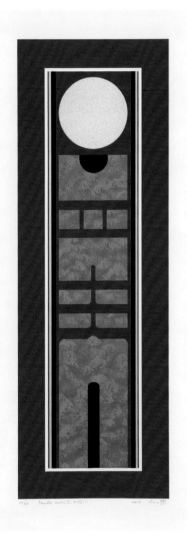

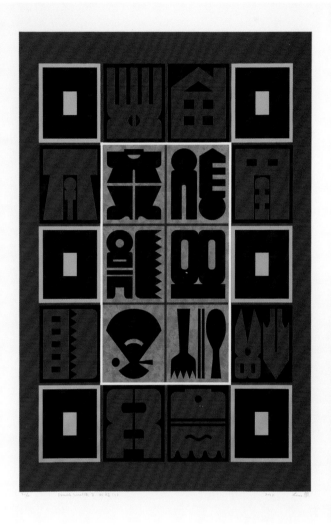

四季一二三四

Four Seasons I II III IV

絲網版
Silkscreen
91×29cm ×4
1997

國立臺灣美術館典藏

月下雅集

Gathering under The Moonlight

絲網版
Silkscreen
54×81cm
1992

4/25　　　　　　　　　Gathering under the moon light　月下雅集　　　　　　　1992　Liao 廖

春之門

Gate of Spring

絲網版
Silkscreen
47×62cm
1992

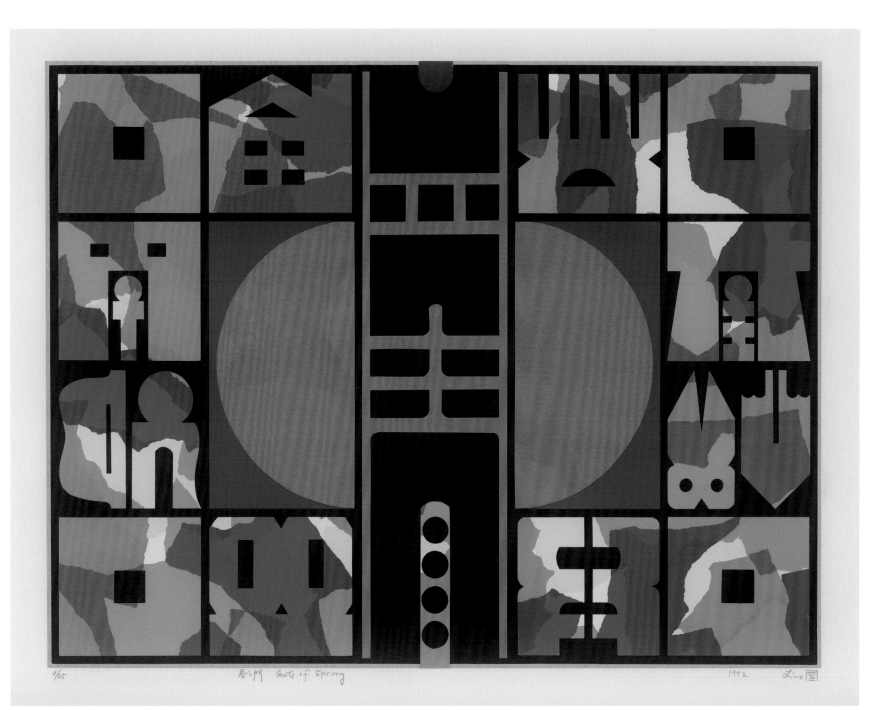

9/25   春之門 Gate of Spring   1992   Liao 廖

園中雅聚 # 10

Garden Party # 10

絲網版 . 紙凹版 . 金屬蝕刻
Silkscreen & Collagraph & Etching
54×81cm
1992

4/20   Garden party #10　圖中雅集－10   1992

敘園（二）

Rendez Vous in A Garden Ⅱ

絲網版、紙凹版
Silkscreen & Collagraph
43×60cm
1991

11/20 　　　茶園 (二) Rendezvous in a garden II 　　　　　　　1991 　Liao 廖

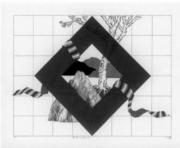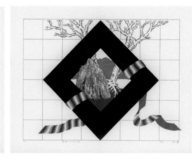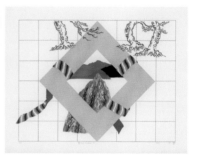

窗（春）（夏）（秋）（冬）

Window I II III IV

絲網版、紙凹版
Silkscreen & Collagraph
43×58cm ×4
1989

窗（春）

Window I ｜ 絲網版、紙凹版 Silkscreen & Collagraph ｜ 43×58cm ｜ 1989

台北市立美術館典藏

窗（夏）
Window II ｜ 絲網版、紙凹版 Silkscreen & Collagraph ｜ 43×58cm ｜ 1989

台北市立美術館典藏

窗（秋）
Window Ⅲ ｜ 絲網版、紙凹版 Silkscreen & Collagraph ｜ 43×58cm ｜ 1989

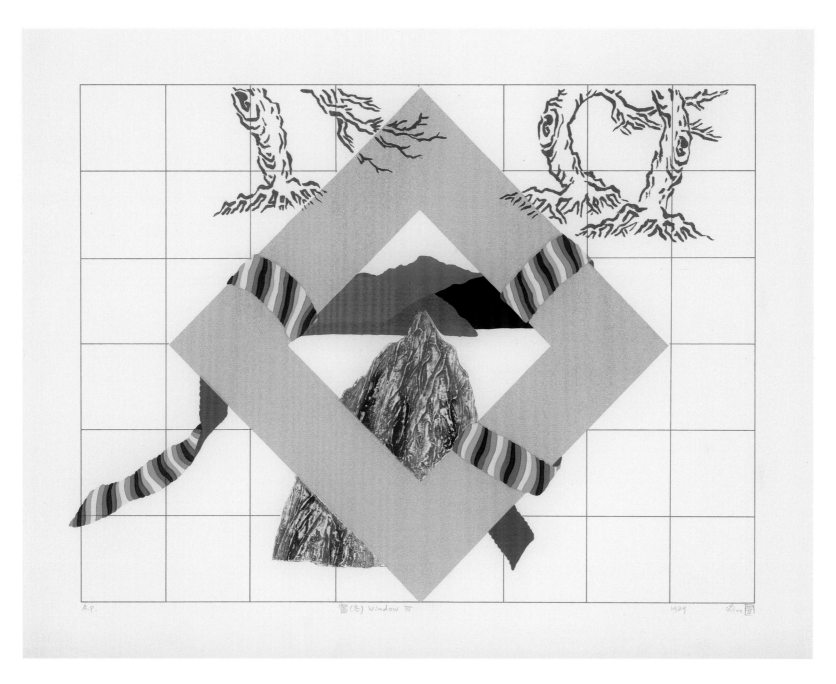

窗（冬）

Window Ⅳ｜絲網版、紙凹版 Silkscreen & Collagraph｜43×58cm｜1989

台北市立美術館典藏

山 湖 竹 Ⅰ Ⅱ Ⅲ

Mountains/Lake/Bamboo Ⅰ Ⅱ Ⅲ

絲網版、紙凹版
Silkscreen & Collagraph
44×58cm ×3
1987

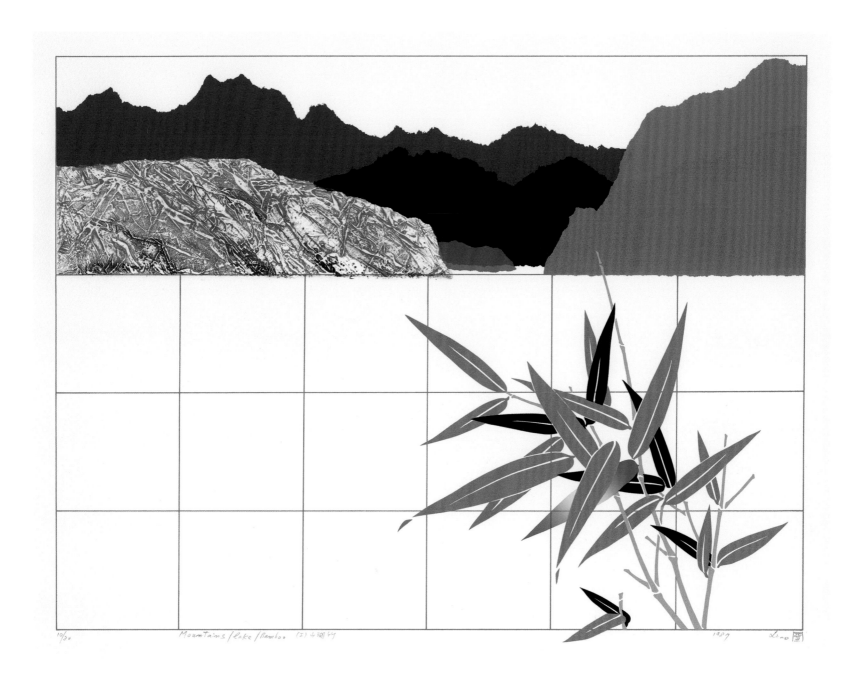

山 湖 竹 I

Mountains/Lake/Bamboo I | 絲網版、紙凹版 Silkscreen & Collagraph | 44×58cm | 1987

台北市立美術館典藏

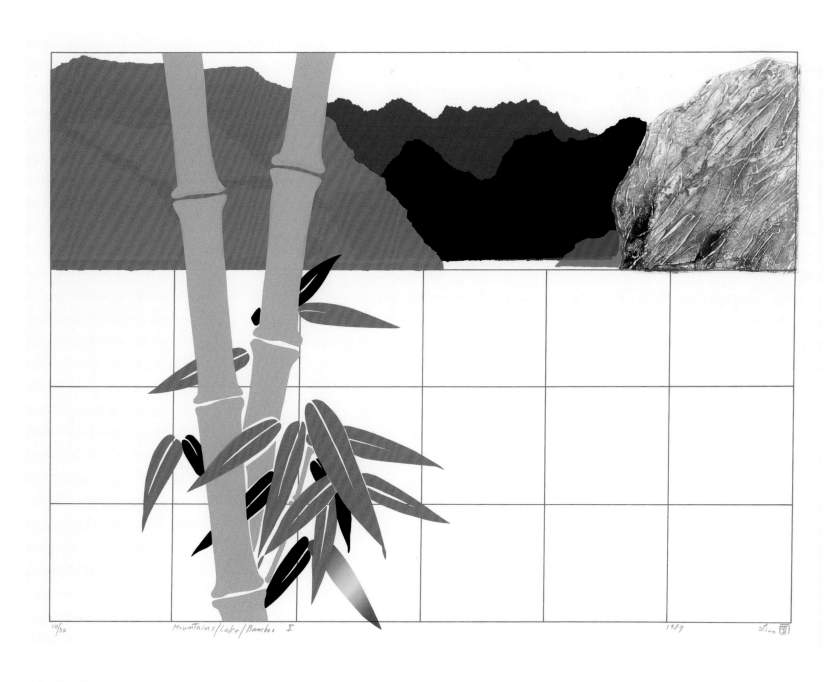

山　湖　竹 II
Mountains/Lake/Bamboo II ｜ 絲網版、紙凹版 Silkscreen & Collagraph ｜ 44×58cm ｜ 1987

10/50   Mountains / Lake / Bamboo III.   1987

山 湖 竹 Ⅲ
Mountains/Lake/Bamboo Ⅲ ｜ 絲網版、紙凹版 Silkscreen & Collagraph ｜ 44×58cm ｜ 1987

捉影

Drawing

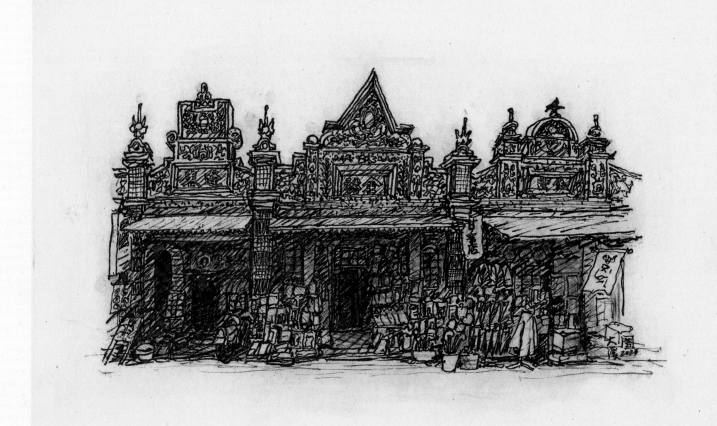

A.P.   老街 Old Street   2021   Liao 圖

老街

Old Street

金屬蝕刻
Etching
27×39.5cm
2021

小南門 Little South Gate 2021

小南門

Little South Gate

金屬蝕刻
Etching
27×39.5cm
2021

AP.　　　　龍山寺 Lung Shan Temple　　　　　2021　　　Liao 图

龍山寺

Longshan Temple

金屬蝕刻
Etching
27×39.5cm
2021

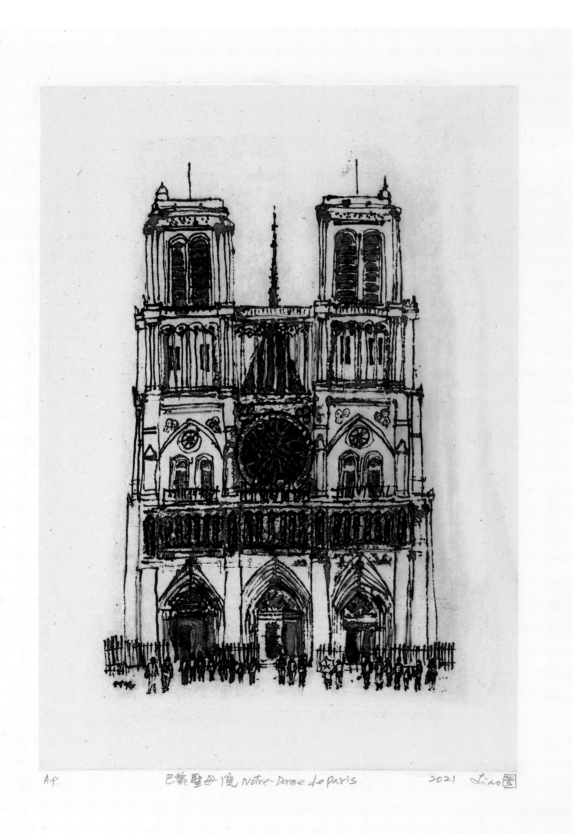

A.P.　　　巴黎聖母院 Notre-Dame de Paris　　　2021　Liao

巴黎聖母院

Notre-Dame de Paris

金屬蝕刻
Etching
41×28.5cm
2021

簡歷＿＿＿＿＿＿

Liao 区

個展（節選）_____

2021 ●「廖修平：跨越疆界的最前線」，台
南市美術館，台南，台灣

2019 ●「樸素高貴：廖修平的藝術歷程」，
尊彩藝術中心，台北，台灣
●「樸素高貴：廖修平的藝術歷程」，
奕思畫廊，中環，香港
●「廖修平的藝術：跨域‧多元藝術」，
馬來西亞國家美術館，吉隆坡

2018 ●「樸素的符號‧高貴的美感：廖修平
繪畫展 2000-2018」，龍門畫廊，黃竹
坑，香港

2016 ●「福彩‧版華 — 廖修平之多元藝
道」，國立歷史博物館，台北
●「Masterpiece Room — 廖修平作品
展」，國立臺北藝術大學關渡美術館，
台北

2015 ●「符號藝術—廖修平創作展」，台灣
國際創價學會，宜蘭 花蓮 台東

2014 ●「福華人生—廖修平個展」，福華沙
龍，台北
●「版‧畫‧交響—廖修平創作歷程
展」，高雄市立美術館，台灣

2013 ●「跨域‧典範—廖修平的真實與虛
擬」，中華文化總會，台北，台灣

2012 ●「界面‧印痕—廖修平與臺灣現代版
畫之發展」，國立臺灣美術館，台灣
●「臺灣現代版畫先行者—廖修平個
展」，行天空附設圖書館，台北，台灣

2011 ●「版畫人生」—廖修平教授藝術創作
特展，國立臺灣師範大學圖書館一樓大
廳，台北，台灣
●「廖修平作品展—門」，大同大學志

生紀念館，台北，台灣

2011 ●「台灣現代版畫的播種者—廖修
平」，紐約雀兒喜美術館，美國

2010 ●「文化尋根 建構台灣美術百年史」，
創價文化藝術系列展覽—
●「台灣現代版畫播種者—廖修平個
展」，台灣創價學會藝文中心巡迴展

2009 ●「福華人生–廖修平作品展」，北京
中國美術館，中國
●「廖修平作品展」，東京澀谷區立松
濤美術館，日本

2007 ●「符號人生‧夢境系列」，台北國父
紀念館，台灣

2001 ●「門和四季之敘系列」，舊金山中華
文化中心，美國
●「版畫師傅–廖修平版畫回顧展」，
國立歷史博物館，台北，台灣

2000 ● 香港藝術中心，中國，香港
●門戶之「鑑」–廖修平的符號藝術，
台北市立美術館，台灣

1998 ● 巴黎國際藝術城，法國

1997 ● 西格瑪畫廊，紐約，美國

1994 ● 台北福華沙龍，台灣

1993 ● 上海美術館，中國

1992 ● 烈日市立現代美術館，比利時
● 台灣省立美術館，台灣，台中

1991 ● 江蘇省立美術館，中國，南京

1990 ● 紐約蘇河區喜格瑪畫廊，美國

1989 ● 台北市立美術館，台灣

1986 ● 新澤西州紐瓦克公立圖書館，美國

1984 ● 東京松屋畫廊，日本
● 雷廷根雷市立美術館，德國

1983 ● 高雄市立文化中心，台灣

1982 ● 國立歷史博物館（國家畫廊），台灣
● 洛杉磯辛諾畫廊，美國

1979 ● 東京白田畫廊，日本

1977 ● 新澤西州西東大學藝術中心，美國
● 維州華李大學藝廊，美國
● 札幌克拉克畫廊，日本

1976 ● 省立博物館，台灣

1974 ● 東京小造型畫廊，日本
● 馬德里歐斯馬畫廊，西班牙

1973 ● 舊金山加州榮譽宮殿（版畫部），美國

1972 ● 波士頓亞洲畫廊 美國
● 國立歷史博物館（國家畫廊），台灣

1970 ● 辛辛那提"塔佛托美術館"，美國
● 三集畫廊，香港

1968 ● 比利時那慕文化會館，比利時
● 邁阿密現代美術館，佛州，美國

1967 ● 巴黎青年畫廊，法國
● 巴黎藝術之家，法國

1966 ● 台灣省立博物館，台灣

1964 ● 東京造型畫廊，日本

聯展（節選）

2021
- 「十青現代版畫展」，大墩文化中心大墩藝廊（五），台中，台灣

2020
- 「引藝領潮—1947‧鼓亭莊聯展」，亞洲大學現代美術館，台中，台灣
- 「彼方之境」，問空間，新北，台灣
- 「不均的平面：1957-1983年 面向國際的臺灣版畫」，台南市美術館二館，台南，台灣
- 「台灣美術院十週年院士大展」，國立國父紀念館博愛藝廊，台北；台南市美術館，台南

2019
- 「連結台灣—吳三連獎40 ART聯展」，台南市美術館一館，台南
- 「羅馬尼亞版畫展Tribuna Graphic 2019」，克盧日—納波卡美術館，羅馬尼亞
- 「我在今日：今日畫會60週年展」巡迴展，國立臺灣師範大學德群畫廊、高雄文化中心至眞堂、國立國父紀念館博愛藝廊，台北、高雄
- 「夏日國際版畫展」，曜畫廊，台北，台灣
- 「薩馬拉—台灣版畫藝術三代展」，薩馬拉巴比隆畫廊，俄羅斯
- 「形非勢變—台灣抽象藝術」，大象畫廊，台中，台灣
- 「台南美術館二館開館展：台灣禮讚」，台南市美術館二館，台南，台灣

2018
- 「世界的現代版畫展」，池田記念美術館，新潟，日本
- 「共振‧迴圈：臺灣戰後美術特展」台北國際藝術博覽會，台北

- 「臺灣製造藝術：2018臺灣美術院—馬來西亞展」，創價學會綜合文化中心，吉隆坡，馬來西亞
- 「紙的意象」，福華沙龍，台北
- 「意象符碼」，宛儒畫廊，台北
- 「亞洲當代版畫展在竹縣」，新竹縣政府文化局美術館，新竹
- 「竹風行版：2018現代版畫邀請展」國立清華大學竹師藝術空間，新竹
- 「藏：國際版畫中心收藏展暨廖修平名譽博士作品展」，臺灣師大德群藝廊，台北

2017-18
- 「徬徨之海：旅行畫家‧南風原朝光與台灣、沖繩」，沖繩縣立博物館美術館，日本

2017
- 「聚‧火：鶯歌、上海、紐約三城彩瓷創作聯展」臺華藝術中心，台北，台灣
- 「心傳：臺灣‧西班牙版畫交流展」，亞億藝術空間，台北
- 「今日画展」，國立國父紀念館，台北，台灣
- 「台灣製造藝術：2017台灣美術院院士大展」，國立國父紀念館，台北

2016
- 「人間‧山水：藝術創作邀請展」，羅東文化工廠2F天空藝廊，宜蘭
- 「版圖擴張—緣聚廖修平」巡迴展，台南、高雄、屏東、桃園
- 「紙上創作—台日韓美術交流展」，新營文化中心，台南市
- 「台灣製造藝術：2016台灣美術院海外展—韓國」，大韓民國藝術院美術

館，首爾，韓國

2015-16
- 「無邊‧無界：台法藝術交流展」，國路紀念館中山畫廊，台北；法國泰勒基金會展廳，巴黎

2015
- 「畫家畫金門 寫生紀行」，福華沙龍，台北
- 「精華匯聚：2015宜蘭國際版畫邀請展」，宜蘭美術館，台灣
- 「集十傑之長‧創台灣之光」第二屆全國十大傑出青年美術創作得主巡迴展，台北國父紀念館，台灣
- 「凹凸有誌印痕歲月—台灣50現代版畫展」，築空間，台北，台灣

2014-15
- 「美好今日：今日畫會今日展2014-2015巡迴展」，高雄、桃園、台北、宜蘭，台灣

2014
- 「2014高雄藝術博覽會」，高雄翰品酒店，高雄
- 「抽象‧符碼‧東方情—台灣現代藝術巨匠大展」，尊彩藝術中心，台北
- 「いま台灣」台灣美術院聯展，東京澀谷區立松濤美術館，日本
- 「臺灣 製造 美術」，臺灣美術院澳洲國家大學展覽，澳洲國家大學畫廊

2013
- 「美麗台灣—台灣近現代名家經典作展」，北京中國美術館，上海中華藝術宮
- 「台灣50現代畫展」，築空間，台北，台灣
- 「現代‧迭起—2013台灣的當代藝術」，國立國父紀念館，台北，台灣
- 「台灣美術家刺客列傳‧二年級

生 ·1931-1940」國立台灣美術館，台中，台灣

●「第一屆澳門版畫三年展」，澳門南灣舊法院大樓

2012 ●「Prints Tokyo 2012-International Print Exhibition Tokyo 2012」，東京都美術館，日本

●「非形之形─台灣抽象藝術」，台北市立美術館，台北

●「原點的維度── 2012 年上海國際版畫展」，上海美術館，中國

●「後殖民與後現代 台灣美術院士第二屆大展」，國立國父紀念館，台北，台灣

●「繼往開來」臺灣、韓國國際版畫交流展，台北、台中、台南、高雄

●「國美 無雙」館藏精品常設展，國立臺灣美術館，台中，台灣

2011 ●「藝林鼎足─朱爲白、廖修平、李錫奇」，國立國父紀念館，台北，台灣

●「百歲百畫－台灣當代畫家邀請展」，國立國父紀念館，台北，台灣

●「開創 · 交流」台灣美術院院士作品大陸巡迴展，北京中國美術館，廣州廣東美術館，中國

●「SKY － 2011 亞洲 版／圖 展」，國立臺北藝術大學關渡美術館，台北，台灣

2010 ●「傳承與開創」台灣美術院美術院士首屆大展，國立國父紀念館，台北，台灣

●「百年華人繪畫大觀 · 世界巡迴大展」，長流美術館，台灣、北京、上海、日本、美國、法國

●「續」李仲生現代繪畫獎特展，國立台灣美術館，台中，台灣

●「異象──典藏抽象繪畫展」，國立台灣美術館，台中，台灣

2009 ●「60 年代旅巴黎台灣畫家展」，國立國父紀念館，台北，台灣

●「講 · 述：2009 海峽兩岸當代藝術展」，國立台灣美術館、中國北京美術館

2008-09 ●「今日畫會 今日畫展」，今日畫會 2008~2009 巡迴展，桃園、台中、新竹、彰化、台北、高雄

2008 ●「台灣現代美術的先驅」，馬利蘭州陶森大學亞洲文化藝術中心，美國

●「台灣藝術 · 當代演繹」，國立摩拉維亞美術館，捷克

●「2008 年亞太國際版畫邀請展暨學術研討會」，台北國父紀念館，台灣

2007-08 ●歷史的光輝－全省美展六十回顧展，國立台灣美術館，台灣

●全國十大傑出青年美術創作得主巡迴展，台北國父紀念館，台灣

2007 ●「2007 世紀初藝術－－海峽兩岸繪畫聯展」，北京

2006 ●第五屆埃及國際版畫三年展，埃及

●台灣美術－現代巨匠東京五人展，相田光男美術館，日本

●版畫藝術－中日韓現代版畫展，首爾 Milal Museum of Art，韓國

2005 ●釜山國際版畫雙年展，韓國

2004 ●「版畫東西交流之波展」─日本東京 ISPA 國際版畫藝術論壇暨邀請展，東京藝術大學，東京都町田市版畫藝術館，日本

2003 ●新世紀版畫特展，國立台灣藝術教育館，台灣

2001 ●「千濤拍岸──台灣美術一百年」，國立台灣美術館，台灣

●「台北現代藝術本位與對話」聯展，上海美術館，中國

2000 ●「2000 年國際版畫邀請展」暨學術研討會，台灣，日本

●克勞可國際版畫三年展，波蘭

1999 ●「日台版畫交流展」，東京都目黑區立美術館，日本

1998 ●「第二屆國家文藝獎得獎者展覽」，台北市立美術館、高雄市立美術館，台灣

1996 ●「台灣藝術主體性」1996 台北雙年展，台灣

1993 ●「中國當代繪圖展」，國立明斯克美術館，白俄羅斯

●挪威國際版畫三年展，挪威

1991 ●當代版畫大展「台北─北京」，北京，中國

1989 ●挪威國際版畫三年展，挪威

1988 ●「中國現代版畫展」，日本町田市立國際版畫美術館，日本

1978 ●「中韓現代版畫展」，漢城，韓國；台北，台灣

1977 ●「中國現代版畫展」，紐約聖若望大學，美國

聯展（節選）

收藏機構（節選）

● 國立台灣美術館
● 台北市立美術館
● 高雄市立美術館
● 香港藝術館
● 中國上海美術館
● 北京中國美術館
● 日本國立東京近代美術館
● 韓國漢城國立現代美術館
● 英國倫敦大英帝國博物館
● 英國倫敦維多利亞阿爾伯特美術館
● 比利時烈日市立現代美術館
● 西班牙馬德里當代藝術館
● 奧地利維也納阿爾博蒂那博物館
● 美國紐約大都會博物館
● 以色列海華現代美術館

● 2020 造訪桃園地景藝術節

● 2019年在尊彩個展和海洋畫會員及味岡義人合影

Resume _____

BIOGRAPHY

1936	Born in Taiwan
1959	Graduated from National Taiwan Normal University, Fine Arts B.A.
1962~64	Continued his studies at Tokyo University of Education, Japan.
1965~6	Studied at L'ecole des Beaux-Arts, Paris, France under R. Chastel and at Atelier 17 under S. W. Hayter
1969	Moved to New York City, U.S.A.
1973~76	Returned to Taiwan and taught printmaking at National Taiwan Normal University, Chinese Culture University and National Taiwan Academy of Arts
1977-79	Invited by Tsukuba University, Japan to set up a printmaking workshop and taught there for two and half years.
1979-92	Adjunct professor of Arts at Seton Hall University in New Jersey for 12 years.
2002	Moved back to Taiwan and focus on painting and printmaking creations. Teaching printmaking at Taipei National University of Arts, Taiwan University of Arts, and Taiwan Normal University, Department of Continuing Education (Master of Arts Program)
2009-20	Director of Taiwan Academy of Fine Arts
2009 to present	Chair Professor at National Taiwan Normal University.
2021	Honorary Director of Taiwan Academy of Fine Arts.

SOLO EXHIBITIONS

2021	"LIAO: Frontline/ Frontier",Tainan Art Museum, Tainan, Taiwan, R.O.C.
2019	"The Art of Liao Shio-Ping:Cross Region・Diverse approaches", National Art Gallery, Malaysia.
2016	"Vivid Colors・Vigorous Life：Liao Shiou-Ping, a Mixed Media Retrospective", National Museum of History, , Taipei, Taiwan, R.O.C.
2014	"A Symphony of Printmaking and Painting: The Art of Liao Shiou-Ping", Kaohsiung Museum of Fine Arts, Taiwan, R.O.C.
2011	"The Pioneer of Modern Printmaking in Taiwan–Liao Shiou-Ping", Chelsea Art Museum, New York City, U.S.A.
2009	"Exhibition of Art Works by Liao Shiou Ping", National Art Museum Of China, China.
	"Liao Shiou-Ping Solo Exhibition", The Shoto Museum of Art, Tokyo, Japan.

GROUP EXHIBITIONS

2021	"2021 Evergreen Modern Graphic Art Exhibition" Dadun Gallery(V), Taichung City Dadun Cultural Center, Taiwan, R.O.C.
2020	"Uneven Horizons1957-1983:The Internationalist Taiwanese Printmaking Tainan Art Museum", Tainan Art Museum, Tainan, Taiwan, R.O.C.
2018	"International Contemporary Print", Ikeda Art Museum, Niigata, Japan.
2014	"Art of Made in Taiwan (MIT)" An Exhibition from the Taiwan Academy of Fine Arts, School of Art Gallery Australian National University, Australia.
2013	"Modernity, the Ever-rising New Wave-Taiwan Contemporary Art 2013", National Dr. Sun Yat-sen Memorial Hall, Taipei, Taiwan, R.O.C.
2012	"Dimensions of Origin – the 2nd shanghai International Printmaking Exhibition 2012" Shanghai Art Museum, Shanghai.

AWARDS

2018	Honorary Degree of Doctor of Philosophy in Fine Arts, Awarded by National Taiwan Normal University.
2010	The 29th National Cultural Award, Taiwan
2006	Honorary prize of the 5th Egyptian International Print Triennial Exhibition, Egypt
1998	National Literature and Art Achievement Award, Taiwan
1993	Silver Medal, Norwegian International Print Triennial, Norway.

COLLECTION

The Metropolitan Museum of Art, New York, U.S.A./British Museum, London, U.K.
Musée d'Art Moderne de la Ville de Paris, France/National Museum of Modern Art, Tokyo, Japan
National Museum of contemporary Art, Seoul, Korea/Shanghai Art Museum, Shanghai, China
Taipei Fine Arts Museum, Taiwan, R.O.C./National Taiwan Museum of Fine Arts, Taiwan, R.O.C

國家圖書館出版品預行編目（CIP）資料

季節歲月：廖修平作品集 = Life's season : the art
 works of Liao Shiou-Ping / 廖修平著作. -- 初版. --
桃園市：桃園市政府文化局，民 110.10
　　面；　公分
　ISBN 978-626-7020-32-6(平裝)

　1. 版畫 2. 畫冊

937　　　　　　　　　　110015479

季 節 歲 月

Life's Season -
The Art Works of Liao Shiou-Ping

季節歲月—廖修平作品集

著 作 者 ｜ 廖修平
指導單位 ｜ 桃園市議會、桃園市政府
主辦單位 ｜ 桃園市政府文化局
協辦單位 ｜ 財團法人福修文化藝術基金會
　　　　　　台北市大安區仁愛路 4 段 2 號 3 樓　02-27028515
發 行 人 ｜ 莊秀美
出 版 者 ｜ 桃園市政府文化局
　　　　　　桃園市桃園區縣府路 21 號　03-3322592
執行編輯 ｜ 郭俊麟、黃妃珊、張麗齡
封面題字 ｜ 程代勒
企劃統籌 ｜ 張愛青、王永嘉
美術設計 ｜ 張玉穎
印 　 刷 ｜ 秀立設計印刷有限公司　02-25969366
出版日期 ｜ 中華民國 110 年 10 月（初版）
定 　 價 ｜ 500 元
I S B N ｜ 978-626-7020-32-6
G P N ｜ 1011001428

版墨
交融
Fusion of the
Printmaking and Ink Art